Exile at Sarzana

OTHER BOOKS BY LAURA BRYLAWSKI-MILLER

Novels

The Square at Vigevano
(2000, Washington Writers' Publishing House)

The Medusa's Smile
(2006, Washington Writers' Publishing House)

The Shadow of the Evening
(2010, Eloquent Books)

Poetry

The Snow on Lake Como
(1991, Washington Writers' Publishing House)

SARZANA: a small town at the Tuscan-Ligurian border where Guido Cavalcanti was exiled from Florence for political reasons in 1300.

EXILE AT SARZANA

LAURA BRYLAWSKI-MILLER

BRP
Broadkill River Press

EXILE AT SARZANA
Copyright © 2010 Laura Brylawski-Miller
All rights reserved.
Printed in the United States of America.

COVER DESIGN	Sid Gold & Barbara Shaw
AUTHOR PHOTOGRAPH	Brandon Brylawski
TYPESETTING AND LAYOUT	Barbara Shaw

Library of Congress Control Number: 2010932702
ISBN 978-0-9826030-5-5

BRP
Broadkill River Press

James C.L. Brown,
Publisher
Broadkill River Press
104 Federal Street,
Milton, Delaware 19968
E-mail: the_broadkill_press@earthlink.net

To George

ACKNOWLEDGMENTS

Grateful acknowledgments are due to the editors of the following journals in which these poems first appeared, some in different form

Folio: Fog

Hungry as We Are WWPH Anthology: The King of a Rainy Country; The Stars of the Bear

The Potomac Review: Volterra; Fly Fishing, Lake Como; Thinking of You on a March Morning

WPFW 89.3 FM Poetry Anthology: Street Musicians, Lucca

CONTENTS

1. ELEMENTS

"Like Snow on a Windless Alp" • 3
After the Carnival • 4
Volterra • 6
Street Musicians, Lucca • 8
Meson del Coso • 9
View of Toledo • 11
Untitled • 12
End of Day • 13
San Babila, Milan • 14
Fishtail Lodge, Pokhara • 15
Driving in Nepal • 16
Sky Burial • 18
The Castle • 19
Summer in the Museum Garden • 21
Requiem for a Poker Player • 22
Homage to Verlaine • 23
The Inmates • 25
Pavane for a Dead Princess • 26
Castles in Air • 27
The Stars of the Bear • 28
Opals • 30
Snow White • 31
The King of a Rainy Country • 33
Crossing Key Bridge on Foot • 35
Wisteria • 36
Weekend in Paris (Virginia) • 38

2. SHADOWS

    Fog • 43
    Via Cerva • 44
    March Storm • 46
    Thinking of You, on a March Morning • 47
    Three Chinese Poems • 48
    Winters • 50
    Visit to Ravello • 51
    Elegy • 53
    Arrivederci • 54
    St. Ambrose Square • 56
    Blue Elegy • 58
    Marrons Glacés • 59
    Luna Parks • 61
    For Brendan • 64

3. EXILE AT SARZANA

    Fly fishing, Lake Como • 69
    Mallorquin • 71
    Monterosso • 72
    To Guido Cavalcanti • 74
    Scuba • 76
    Ocean City • 78
    Memorial Day, Cape May 2007 • 81
    The Shape of Water • 83
    Migrants • 84
    36 New Aspects of Ghosts • 86
    Kismet • 87
    Of Saints and Snows • 88
    Going Back • 90
    Letter to Yang Chen Chai • 91
    Opera Ball at the German Embassy • 92

ELEMENTS

"LIKE SNOW ON A WINDLESS ALP"

As I leave the Italian Store
—a ciabatta, fresh mozzarella-
it begins to snow. Large
weightless flakes drift down
from an infinite sky in a white silence
that mutes the traffic on Lee Highway, dims
the bright neon of the pawnbroker's shop.
I stand there in the cold, errands
forgotten as a line by Dante
blooms up from far recesses
of high-school memory: "*Come di neve
in alpe senza vento.*" For a moment
time is erased. That windless snow
now descends quietly on us both,
the same flakes melting on our skin
as we pause to look up at a gray nothing
that unites us, him in a bitter winter
at Ravenna, surviving on the salty
bread of exile, and me exiled here
among parked cars, clutching
this stylish food that he too ate,
bridged through the centuries between us
by the circular mystery of existence.

AFTER THE CARNIVAL

All that is left by morning
of the cloud-glory of the cherry tree
is a soiled handful of confetti
flung on the pavement
by a profligate rain. The end
of Carnival. Revelers have gone
And Lent tolls purple
in the frigid air.

Now a dark spring
urges the withered branches,
fools ghostly primulas
to bloom along the stream.
Tidy violets, disheveled
dandelions re-surge unwary.

But too many lost
Aprils engulf me, a cold sea
tugs at the mind with undertows
from consumed existences.
Rain drips from the magnolia
relentless as the drop
in the clepsydra—
faces and voices
glide slowly into oblivion.

Where have the revelers
gone? Their white masks
disguise nothing but air.

Still, greedy as newborn
bright plumes emerge

from the sycamore. Green
summer will come,
hide the cherry's scars.

VOLTERRA

The fields mount toward the rock
in yellow-green swells—a tide
of wheat stubbles, olive leaves
rushes up to menace walls that flee
heavenwards. You think of Titans
and assaults to the sky.
Or, maybe, Saint Augustine.

A city like a well, the same
elemental sufficiency: stone,
hidden water. Even the pool
at the hotel seems a cistern,
hoarded, ready for a siege. A black
scissor-tailed swallow
sweeps down to drink, soars,
sweeps across the pool again,
becomes a messenger, the winged
arrow over the wall that signals
take heart, help is on the way.
But down below in the plain
an army of sunflowers
turns ruffled heads away.
They will not come.

In the kiln of the sun
rooftops bleach to the bones
of long-dead summers—you hear
the sand flow in the hourglass.
But time is not an adversary,
here. A flowerpot shard crumbles
under your sandal, terracotta dust
reshapes itself into a primal form:
an earlier sun beats down, July

has yet no name and an Etruscan girl
dips water from a jar under the black
shade of a plum tree. She smiles
the smile of those who know
and won't tell.

What did they know, these Etruscans
so hooked on Hades
they scrambled to get there
any which way, foot, chariot,
boat. Why this nostalgia
for the deep cool earth,
its mossy silence?
You watch them lounge
on their sarcophagi
as if on stony sofas,
serene, fulfilled,
perusing entrails
like a daily horoscope.
But one looks straight
at you, eyes of a satyr,
and thin lips bow upwards.

At sunset, in the piazza
old men gather, sit on stone
benches by the duomo: they've always
been here, like the stones,
the swallows, this purple
vespertine sky. But sand
glides in the hourglass
and you are the sand. Down
below, the horizon exiles the sun.

STREET MUSICIANS, LUCCA

The Peruvian boys dance
in a circle, a slight
syncopation
in their step
a vestige
of ritual rhythms
undulated
as the sweet
reedy music
thin as Andean
air pierces
the Tuscan evening
with alien longings
of migratory birds
stranded across oceans
across seasons
to this street
in the heat
of Lucca in July.

MESON DEL COSO
Alicante

Fernando
bailaor flamenco,
eyes of a woman betrayed,
disdain of centuries
in the mouth,
make-up stains
on the frills of his shirt.
A lean, hungry boy,
maricon,
who dreams of Hollywood
while a turista
at the back table
dreams of Spanish dancers.
Murky longings
twang from a guitar.
Olé, we cry
as we eat *caracoles*,
spear tired olives
with banderillas.
"*Quando un hombre
me penetra*" Fernando whispers
"*yo siento como una mujer.*"
Tomorrow
the sun will rise,
tonight we live
in borrowed skin.
So cry me a river
of sangria,
let the guitar's
pulse fill the blood.
The meson's owner
is named Jesus.

Maybe
we will be saved.

VIEW OF TOLEDO
(El Greco)

Where are the people
who strolled along the bridge
on summer nights—sinewy
young men, a black-shawled girl
with downcast eyes
and a rose in her hair?

The river has become
a dead man's mirror,
reflects a sky
of crucifixion.
Albatross clouds sweep down,
hover above the towers.

Blind houses crackle
in the storm, fluoresce blue.
Outside the walls
exiled trees wait.

And the Alcazar, yet to come.

UNTITLED

This
is for that spidery
red kitten
at the *celler*
in Pollenza
who ate my fish
then slept
outflung
on the curve
of my thigh,
weightless
shared warmth
remembered more
than the faces
of men who loved me
and begged
for the same privilege.

END OF DAY
Attilio Simonetti
(Barbizon School, ca. 1890)

February. The month of dirty snow
and grey souls. Evening. Slow
homeward trudge along a country road
rutted by carts—slush seeping in,
shackling exhausted feet.
Silhouettes of houses at the horizon
hold no promise of warmth. Black
gibbet trees blur the edge of dusk.

But high above
a vampire sunset glows
with winter fire, drains
all life from the land,
inflames the puddles
with fragments of some high Eldorado,
a *Civitas Dei* no one can reach
but it's there. Ask your grief
to be wise. The day is ending—
see, dark rest will come.

SAN BABILA—MILAN

Noon. In Piazza San Babila
a girl, small face as crumpled
as the tissue in her hand,
is crying on a young man's
shoulder. He pats her back
turning away from time to time
so he won't blow smoke
in her face. Because she's crying
and he smokes. "Tell me
the truth," she pleads,
but he just pats her back
and says nothing. For
who really wants Truth
emerging naked from her well,
not Pontius Pilate, forever
washing his hands, not
the man wasting away
at the hospice, not this girl
who only wishes back
yesterday's lies. So
he lights another cigarette,
she dries her eyes
and they go on in silence
while the truth dissolves
in the noon air, ephemeral
as the smoke he won't
give up, the promises
he could not keep.

FISHTAIL LODGE, POKHARA
(Nepal)

Someone out on the lake
is playing "Fur Elise"
on a flute. Can music
make landscapes alien
to themselves, exile
that tree by the raft landing
like the Tibetan refugees
hawking beads in its shade,
their need our daily gauntlet?
We cross on the lodge raft
at will, an easy glide
between two worlds—no
question of salvation
here: limpid waters,
no Charon, a flute.

Why then the unbidden
asp in the reeds:
how shall we answer
for the dispossessed
and save ourselves?
As to the armless boy
watching us click
our cameras (who dressed him
in that striped shirt,
who feeds him?) his silence
weighs like a judgement.
Out on the lake
you can hear his ghost hands
playing that flute. No,
we will not save ourselves.

DRIVING IN NEPAL

I

What at the sight
of our approaching van
impels people—and dogs—
to cross the road?
Through glass, eyes meet
in an unequal recognition,
a sudden smile forgives all.
We drive on—our guilt
mingles with the dust in the air.

II

A child with a perfect face
stands in a shack's doorway,
her dress the color
of withered hyacinths.
The road might take her
away to be a burnt bride
in a far village; or maybe
she will waste here, faded
like her blue dress
from too much use.
She watches
as we go by,
with the silence
of those left behind.

III

Midday, in a small town
we drove through bicycles
as through a swarm of insects.
Wheels, handlebars—shimmering
dragonflies' wings—flashed
by the windshield, smiles
teasing our easy fears,
then exploded away, dissolved
in white noon light,
flew straight into the the sun.

SKY BURIAL
Tibet

The *Assumption of the Virgin*
painted by Titian in the Frari church
holds no more mystery that this
sublimation by vulture, this ultimate
recycling: disappear, consumed
by creatures born of this hypnotic
sky—bluer than any heaven
you could hope for—flesh
lacerated, bones crushed to a meal
to feed the hungry. Surely
an act of mercy recorded, a last chance
to do some good. And surely
better than putrefaction, slow
decay to a few trace minerals
for nourishing wild flowers
that couldn't grow here anyway.
Fire? It would release toxic
thoughts, pollute the crystal air.
No, far better this renewed
tie to Prometheus. Imagine him
unbound, redeemed, ascending
among fierce-beaked, taloned
dark-winged angels.

THE CASTLE
To K., the Land Surveyor

I

Perhaps your strength was innocence,
the fool's charmed armor. Maybe
it was submerged remembrance of
a previous time, when clearer eyes
could read the Runic pitting
on ice-cracked boulders, divine
a future cast like molten lead
by tangled winter branches
on moonlit snow. And perhaps
when you stopped for a moment
on the bridge and looked up,
it was just faith—the belief
in a promise given long ago
and reneged on the way: there is
a meaning to the voyage—hope
cannot be a sin to be expiated.

II

It is always deepest winter,
always evening, when we reach
that unnamed village blanketed
in snow. Huddled, silent houses,
where few windows glow secret
like banked embers. We sense
the castle in the void above,
in the doorless grey fog that mutes
our steps, dissolves in mist
the lifeline of the traveled road
at our back. It's a bitter
cold night, and we come from nothing.

Did Franz echo here winters in Prague,
a castle that cuts into thin air,
severs the bond between earth and sky?
Is this the longing that impelled you—
and us—to this place? Are we your kin,
exiles in our own skin, exiles
from a country we don't know?

III

Sunset flames leaded windows
makes the village houses blind.
The Castle holds impervious. No
message comes, no password. There's
no thaw here, no hope of spring,
the sky is a glass bell
where voices mute and die.
Eyes look away. We are
danger, we who won't give up.

VI

We won't give up. Limpid-eyed
as born liars, sharp-eared, full
of tricks, we'll go to earth
in a furrow, become fertile seed
under the snow. Our legs
will intertwine, sink roots
in the dark, secret soil. And there
we'll wait with you. Our stubborn
breaths will mingle, streak the winter air
like a path to the sky, a newborn star.

SUMMER IN THE MUSEUM GARDEN

The bronze boy
stares at the roses
with Aegean eyes.
Around the pond
white peonies
smell of remembered snows.
Layered heat
lulls desires.
Out in the parking lot
cars levitate, dissolve in light.

REQUIEM FOR A POKER PLAYER

Steve McQueen
the Cincinnati Kid
walking at night in the black rain
of a New Orleans of prostitutes,
loneliness dressed in red
in a doorway, the rain's thin wires
suddenly silver in a wedge of light
from a bar, the sizzle
of hot jazz, an old black woman
wailing her blues
at the piano, a web
of lives and now
they're all dead
him and the city
gone with the cancer
and the flood, all gone,
his sharky blue blue eyes
and the gray corpses
floating in the streets
all lost, as we all lose
on the turn of a card
no one sees coming.

HOMAGE TO VERLAINE

Old Story

The smoke stack
by the freeway
it's hardly
Verlaine's palmed tree
but as its pale
smokeleaves unfurl
billow and dive
in the icy
brittle sky
(*si bleu, si calme*)
I too wonder
what have I done
with my youth
what have I done
with last summer's sun.

Autumn

The paper mill's stack against the sky
(*si bleu, si calme*)

remainds me of your tree, its high
swaying palm.

Dark plumes fill the early autumn air,
unfurl and fly

a woman waiting by the Metro stairs
tries not to cry.

I see my lost years in the wind that steals
a dying leaf

I feel the first snow coming to conceal
its unburnt grief.

THE INMATES

Venus in Furs
is in a cage
at the zoo

and we dandle
our aberrations
upon our knees—

unwanted children
cared for
but not loved.

The wall
holding us in
is the fear
in your eyes.

When night comes
we dance barefoot
on shards
of broken dreams.

PAVANE FOR A DEAD PRINCESS
(Ravel)

Don't read hope
in my hand,
it only holds
the gift of my emptiness
masked in the arabesque
of a court dance,
don't read a plea
in the fall of my sleeve,
it only hides
the tugging strings.
I asked no promise
when our eyes
met in the mirror
where I must exist.

But as you watch me leave
this golden room,
sense my warmth
under this shrouding
brocade, trace
my silent mouth
with a healing finger.
I have heard
that skies can be blue.

CASTLES IN AIR

The trick
was in teaching
the stones
to float,
in devising
an invisible mortar
that bound and freed,
like love. The turrets
were easy: they shot up
like rockets
at the four corners
and held.

Yet the dreams
were too heavy.

THE STARS OF THE BEAR
"Vaghe stelle dell'Orsa"
Leopardi

I

November. A huntress moon stalks her prey
across the nitid sky—a small star
freezes, rabbit ensnared by headlight—
looking for a kill, clean and round
and perfect as herself. But the She-Bear
sleeps in another hemisphere tonight,
hibernates in the past as in her cave
of ice—and fears no arrows
nor unleashed remembrance.

II

I'm five, the night of my birthday,
barefoot in the garden and someone
says: "Look! Look at the bears!
Can you see them?" as I search the sky
for a great muzzle, a strong paw
hooking a salmon in the Milky Way
like the bear in my book, who likes
fish and blueberries. But I only
see stars, a thousand galactic fireflies
dancing above my head, a stellar vertigo
rotates in an abyss that sucks me in
so that I must crouch and grasp the grass
by my feet or I shall fall into the sky.
And then I see them, the bear and her cub,
the wondrous menagerie of the void
parade under the big top, starry fur
twinkling electric, heavy body
a-sway with the music of the sphere

around and around, till they merge
in a jumble of stars, disappear
as if it had been all a trick, worse,
a glimpse of Eden. For the first time
I taste exile.

III

And does it ever end, this sensing
that it should have been different,
the fruit not eaten, the right path
easier to recognize? The trees
bore no sign post and the she-wolf,
the lion and the lynx have become
fellow travelers. The *selva oscura*
has gone like the rain forest—soon
there'll be no trees in Madagascar
and Polaris no longer shows the way.
Constellations revolve in horoscopes
in a newspaper—inane promises
eclipsed by the headlines. Time
is a turbulent river sweeping
by, snaring the past in a net of stars,
present and lost like the Great Bear.

OPALS

I like the opal best
because it lives.

Within its depth
glows a caveman's fire,
primordial water bathes
smooth silica boulders,
new-born trees and skies
shimmer with blue and green
fragments of a clear
morning in Eden,
when the world was new.
Then the snake slithers by
purple flecked with gold. Red
flames fill the horizon—Troy
is burning.

In the tilt of a hand
Harlequin comes, wayward
dancer in the snow
of a Venetian winter.
Suddenly, the stone darkens,
a fiery lightning flashes
out of black chaos. Now
the opal rests, smooth
and fragile and cold.
A checkered glass
that holds our world, our story.

I like the opal best
because it dies.

SNOW WHITE

She's Cinderella's dark
German sister, the happy
ending of the story
tainted by poisoned apples,
witches, slaughtered deer's
heart in gold caskets,
murdered gamekeepers,
carved rock-crystal biers
sealed on a hillside
lest ill winds might mark
her undead beauty
through the years. No gory

detail is spared. By contrast
the French girl's lot
holds little to dismay: ashes
yes, but the warmth of evening fire
in snowy winters, fairy
Godmothers turning rags
into ball gowns, pumpkins
to golden coaches, white
prancing horses in a starry night
and, best of all, a tribe
of cheery mice eager to sweep chimneys
and lighten Cindy's load
with mops and brooms and songs,
according to Walt Disney.

For Snow White,
even that happy ending
sounds fishy. Were the dwarfs
forlorn? Misshapen, old,

what did they really feel
toward a straight-limbed
princelin come to steal
their treasure with a kiss?
Were they pretending
when they cheered?
And what about
the gamekeeper and the fawn?

THE KING OF A RAINY COUNTRY

*"Je suis comme le roi
d'un pays pluvieux "*
Baudelaire

In my kingdom where rain
never ending, quiet as a blade
between two ribs, slips in
to quell the surgings of a heart
still unruly, in this palace draped
with ennui like grey silk,
where tarnished mirrors yawn opaque,
stagnant ponds no animal drinks from,
the ladies of the court bare coral breasts
to the crown on my head with avid boredom,
glide into my bed—pearl rosary
smooth and untouched under my fingers,
cool flesh unquenching
as the memory of water.

We embark for cold Cythaeras
that exile the heart, pretend
pastorals in the stables,
change gold to straw. Even
the sad eyes of the horses,
all-accepting, the warm
cloud of their breath can't heal me.

It's then, in the resigned
metronome of rain on the tin roof
that comes the echo of other
possibilities, a distant land
rift with storms and violent sunsets,
burning azures that bleach the earth,

scour it bone-clean. Water there
becomes a lifeline on my hand.
And in that land a woman
with severe brow and quiet eyes,
whom I shall never know,
waits for me, and judges and forgives me.

CROSSING KEY BRIDGE ON FOOT

Always the easy metaphor.
But most bridge crossings
are simply to reach
the other side. No *alea
jacta est*, no rebel eagles
coruscating in the morning sun
along the Rubicon. I'm burning
nothing behind me and the wind
that flows downcurrent unimpeded
just carries gulls—winged
sea-going fantasies of a life
unmoored, of walking on water.

But then, mid-span, the other
lure: how would it feel,
the river rushing up, concrete-
hard, a final knowledge pierced
into the skull by shining spears
of water? The man who abandoned
that dark green car mid-bridge
and jumped—his choice confronts me.

The bridge ends. I dodge
a cyclist, impatient cars
menace on M street. No place
for ghosts. So I'll go on,
leave that drowned driver
to the river, to the mystery
of catfish, of scavenger crabs,
to all that is alive
in the soothing, busy silence
of underwater graves.

WISTERIA

It belongs to another time.
A pergola on a southern lake,
mid-May—let's say 1862—
purple clusters against white
lattice, two girls, a wrought
iron balustrade. You can see
the two heads close together,
smooth hair parted (the line
thin and white as a scar)
to blossom curly above the ears.
One fair, one dark. The fair one,
doe-eyed, slope shouldered
and much admired for a sweet
stupidity (mistakenly perceived
as a non-threat by her suitors)
is talking of the coming ball
but the dark one—who will die
in childbirth in three years—
is lost in the sun-warmed
wisteria sweetness. She dreams
of unknown passions and the grey-
eyed rebel who is marching
with Lee across Virginia
toward Antietam—and will not come back.

Today she would survive, sue
the doctor (the C-scar not quite
perfect, unfit for a bikini)
teeter her days on a balance
beam of child care and career,
wreak restless discontent
on stiff gladiola on a piano bar

and too much time on the internet.
A story of our times. Then
one day, as she fumes impatient
in the rush-hour jam along Lee highway,
she'll glimpse clusters of amethyst
and green, disheveled tendrils clinging
to a tumbled shed behind the Exxon station
and a revenant perfume suddenly
will bless the evening air, awake
a grief for things unknown and gone—
a cause already lost in Eden, in that green
ravine at Antietam, in the daily
defeat of traffic jams
and the long way home.

WEEKEND IN PARIS (VIRGINIA)

A village from a Christmas card.
Inn, church, schoolhouse
lined up as by a child
along a frosty road.
Our room expansive,
crimson-walled, wing chairs
cozying up to a fireplace.
A high brass bed, old prints,
a decanter of port—time past
preserved and reinvented
into bucolic present.
But outside the window
hills and barren trees
are covered with the snows
of yesteryear. Mosby
held meetings here,
there's blood in the earth
under that snow.

Afternoon, we go antiquing
in Middleburg. I buy a gold
mourning locket, for remembrance.

Evening. Snow returns,
swirls in the air. We're held
in thrall inside a glass dome
as we walk to the inn. Candles,
gravlac, a mediocre champagne
and ahi tuna. "Sushi grade"
the haughty waitress proudly
informs us. I think of Mosby

and his Raiders in the snow,
their cold black nights.

The room has become
a warm cocoon. Grey
fireshadows, ghostly
on the crimson walls.
Outside snow descends
on the absurdities of life
in soft, soothing silence.

SHADOWS

FOG

If this morning, as I awoke to a white
invisibility and by a sudden witchcraft
it was Milan's fog out there, that winter
pressing against the window, a pale revenant,

if from that doorless nothing you came back
and a remembered need pierced sharp
and silent, an ambushing blade
sudden against the heart,

if the fog sponged the years away,
ephemeral chalk on a slate,
don't think, love, it's because
I still miss you—I've learned too many

ways to survive. No, perhaps I miss
what I was, that overserious
naive girl who thought to die for love
would have been a good thing. She went

with you in that spellbound winter
and the fog holds you in thrall. I can't
find the sign, the sorcerer's incantation
that will bring you both back or let me go.

VIA CERVA

Perhaps it was the silence of your house
obviously empty but serene, aloof
from the ephemeral fury of rush hour
clogging Via Cerva this evening—like
someone who has stepped ouside events

and managed to bypass change—or maybe
it was looking at your bedroom window
from the outside, the glass so clean,
so hard against this vulnerable sky,
briar rose blurred by poplar pollen

of a too-dry May—a month we never
made love in—but suddenly the old
sense of exile welled up, a silent
flood, unstemmed, uncheckable. It was
as when you stand in San Marco square

and the *acqua alta* seeps up from a drain
and stones and pigeons tremble in amphibious
abiguity. I still don't understand
this hold unfinished things
seem to possess—a barbed hook buried

under the skin, healed over, till a trick
of light reels you back, a window
ripples like an autumn pond disturbed
by a an acorn, gas fumes spiral the air
with the smell of leaves burning—a crow,

long dead, caws in the horn of a car.
Maybe, there is no sense to this,

the long ribbon of years, and who dies
and who goes on.

For surely there is no earthly fairness
to my standing here, reasonably unscathed
and brooding about the meaning of love,
while people are killed in Sarajevo
as they cue for bread. No archduke
this time, only old women, lying
in their black dresses and their blood.

But perhaps, in spite of *panta rei*
and Leonardo and his river, our fate
is simply recurrence. We can't escape
Gavrilo Princip and the carnage of this day
nor the return of blooms on the wisteria,

the snowy afterthought of pollen.
Nor your being still here, my own
beloved living dead, benign Dracula
who comes back when I least expect you,
perennial joker in the pack. It's right

that you should own me again, a girl
etched by time and different loves,
pausing to look at a briar-rose
May in your window while the evening
descends on Via Cerva and on us.

MARCH STORM

The storm that encased naked branches
into spun glass this morning—echoes
of Christmas in Imperial Vienna,
icicle chandeliers, doomed waltzes
at Mayerling with Rudolf and Maria—
has softened into flowers
of snow, a remembered
Majorcan spring: almond groves
in bloom and the new-born sea's
quiet breathing. I had forgotten
that day in March, the steep path
down to a beach where the seaweeds
still held winter's spent fury
in long green fingers, but now
these icy flowers bring it back
and with it you, and the weight
of unmade choices. Suddenly
the past turns as precarious
as tomorrow. Nothing remains.
Those white peacocks we watched
strut raucously on the terrace
at Formentor are ghosts, the flowered
branches retreat barren into winter
and no one knows what is to come.

THINKING OF YOU ON A MARCH MORNING

The day tries to hold on to winter,
but the forsythia is out, trumpets yellow
against the fence. From my window

I watch the breakfast of the birds
in the backyard. Sleet doesn't fool
them. They know what is coming. I drink

my tea and find no need to read
the leaves. I, too, know what's
coming. But like the day, I fear

to lose what's gone. I try to remember
your voice, but too many seasons
have changed guard. Sleet blurs

your face, strands you in a country
we never inhabited, as if you had
been shot at the border while

we tried to escape (some obsolete
cold war, a field still dirty
with March snow) and I had to leave

you there, bleeding through the years
while I went ahead, safe, into a new
country that would not, could not know us.

THREE CHINESE POEMS

WAITING

I'm kneeling on the river bank,
my reflection shimmers in the water.
But I am filled with sadness.
I don't hear your footsteps on the path
and your face
is not mirrored next to mine.
Maybe you'd like to come
but have doubts:
will it be enough,
this quiet house
in the woods by a river?
Or perhaps you fear
no one is waiting?

NOCTURNE

The pillow still holds the imprint of your head,
in the fireplace the flames have died down.
Out in the moonless winter night
cold stars glitter.

LEAVING

I've worked so hard
to to bring beauty into the house.
I've woven fragrant rushes for the rooms
and hung soft yellow lanterns by the door.
Now that you've come
and are resting on the moon-strewn bed,
I am told I don't belong here
and I must leave.
I will go out of the gate one morning,

when frost rims the path with icy flowers.
All that I own
remains here.
On the road I will stop a cart,
ask to be taken far away.
As the cold fields waken
I will lay my head
on my empty hands,
closing my eyes
I'll try not to dream.

WINTERS

You said: "Remember that one day
you will forget me. It's true,
I know," but I was hoarding gestures,
the crinkle around your eyes, even
the dusky silence in the room,
survival harvest for the barren winters
when a wolf-wind would come howling
to sweep cruelly through a house
bereft of us. So many winters gone
since that evening and, you know,
you were wrong. We don't forget
others, we only lose pieces
of ourselves. Your words, the tilt
of your head, even that silence
are still here, untouched.
It's the *me* who loved you,
the one I can't remember.

VISIT TO RAVELLO
for Kay

In the side garden of the hotel
a man was roasting chestnuts.
For a wedding reception, he said
and gave us some: small and sweet
burnt offerings to an archetypal
ritual, a prothalamion for
the garlanded girls of Keats'
Greek urn as they returned to dance
among the secluded lemon groves,
the fierce, stellate mountain laurel
clinging to rock above the sirens' sea.

And soon after we met the wedding party
walking down from the church: the bride
impatient at her groom's clumsy affection
as he straightened a veil whipped by the wind.
A pretty girl, but it didn't augur well.
Then silence, and the first drops of rain.

On that dour December afternoon
Ravello was a forsaken eden: no trace
left of the gilded hordes of summer,
the jet setters lounging by the pool.
Colors eaten by gray. Only in the garden
purple asters defied the coming winter.

We wandered throughout the empty hotel
unseen as ghosts, calling to each other
to feel real, as we opened doors, touched
books, lamps, chairs, to leave
a sign that we had been there,

trespassers in an unguarded paradise.
How we laughed at our impudence,
back safe into the street. We never heard
that other door, opening to the real
Paradise, the voices calling you.

ELEGY

Sadder than the sadness
of losing you
is this tranquil knowing
you really didn't matter—
it goes deeper
than that
the primal flaw
that even love can't cure.
Hope is a rainbow
through a prism,
the deceiving
eye of the hurricane.
You or another failure
it would have been the same.

ARRIVEDERCI

I'm going out
of your life
as if out
of a house
only lived in
for a while,
front door closed
on empty rooms,
memories loaded
on the van
with the sofa,
the kitchen table
with the wobbly leg
we meant to fix
but never did.

In the silence
behind that door,
the house
will hold on
to our presence
in the carpet faded
where the sofa was,
the darker void
left by pictures
on empty walls.

Because we can't
say goodbye
to what we were,
no matter
how many doors

we close, no matter
how many times
we don't look back.

In August 17-19, 1943, the center of
Milan was blanketed by four air
raids that destroyed most of the
area, mainly by fire bombs.

ST. AMBROSE SQUARE
Milan, 1943

He was a frog-eyed, odious bully
the concierge's son at number 4.
In those warm nights in June
as we played in the park by the square
he would invade our games,
pinch arms, yank hair, call us
rich brats, cry babies, try
to pull down our pants and then
promise revenge if we dared to tell.
And laugh. He always had a green
film on his teeth.

The night of that air raid, a star-
filled August, we were at the lake.
The square and the park went up in flames.
The houses torched to eventrated
shells, melted windows stared blind,
a phosphorous sky the only roof.
The fires gutted our past.
But number 4 had taken
a direct hit, the earth opened deep,
became a crater in a barren moon.

They said they dug them out
three days later, lined them up
on the sidewalk like logs, like booty

from a hunt—white eyes upturned
to the ruined sky. Him
too. Bloated, green as a frog.

BLUE ELEGY

       I hate to see
your image
       (the evening sun)
disintegrate
       (go down)
leaving only the blue
blues of the evening,
specter of the rose
haunting the garden.

You were
to be
my perfect grief,
the cleaving absence.
I mourn for my
unbroken heart
singing in the branches,
the taste of water
you left, the oblivious
river closing over you
without a trace,
without a tear.

MARRONS GLACÉS

I hated them, these masterpieces
of confectionary art, bloated
in syrup baths, which would appear
in pastry shops when the first fogs
saddened our autumn. Plump and sleek
pampered odalisques on satin drapes,
they spilled from treasure chests,
piled high in shiny copper cauldrons,
a pyramid adorned with crystallized
violets, the purple petals candied in mid-
beat like tiny, imprisoned butterflies.
In the mouth, they melded to a cloying
paste that stuck to the palate, over-
whelmed taste buds, sent the pancreas
in overdrive. Even gluttons couldn't eat
more than two.

I loved chestnuts, the first, tiny
mountain ones charred over open flame
up at the lake, when late September rain
needled the window, knelled the death
of summer, the return to city and school.
With fingers, tongue turned black by soot,
I would suck the hard kernels, then bite
into a sudden floury sweetness, tinged
with smoke and charcoal—homey,
almost consoling: life would yield
simple answers, and be good.

In town, November brought the bigger
roasted chestnuts, smiling golden
from a slit in the shell. Wrapped

in a newspaper cone they warmed my hands
as I walked home from school in the grey-
red evenings of Milan still torn by war,
the fog like a veil over the silent
eviscerated houses. The belief in simple
answers long gone, but the *caldarroste*
plain and substantial, assuaged hunger
like a kept promise. Their scent erased
the acrid smell of other fires. Those
effete *marrons glacés*, returning safe
in their gilded boxes now seemed alien,
strangers who had not known those flames.

Now they're just
part of the story,
Proustian capsules where a ten year-old
walks in a war-torn city lost in fog.
Still too sweet, but I have learned
to accept artifice. And, oh, those tiny,
candied violets…

In Italy, "Luna Parks" was the generic
name given to itinerant amusement
parks. The English name came, it seems,
from a Victorian one in London.

LUNA PARKS

The story is always written
by the survivors, who can only tell
what didn't happen to them, a negative
reversed space. I was not one of those
children machine-gunned near a carousel,
that's all I know. But forgotten evil
lives on to sink into a heavy void
that maims, and you don't know it.

They would appear in winter,
those Luna Parks, alighting in grey
snowy streets like rainbow-plumed
exotic birds. As a calliope sang tinny
a magic island bloomed out of the fog,
klieg lights sizzled white, raucous
dream barkers rasped their sirens' call.

Suddenly you believed in miracles,
in a world where men ate fire,
swallowed swords, shattered chains
taut around tattooed chest, walked
a blade of hand-to-mouth existence
unscathed. No one knew the ruins
soon to come in bombed houses,
the dead soldiers snared in barbed wire
in the snow, the icy wound
that kills the heartwood
while the leaves still grow.

They were such homey, gentle freaks:
the Fat Lady, smiling in immense deep-
chinned benevolence at the Monkey Boy
as she knitted a green shawl, the Tattooed
Man, with blue cobras writhing on his biceps
but "Mama" curlicued over his heart—
his baby asleep by the caravan.

How far
were the horrors of American side shows,
the phocomelic Seal Boy, the Living Torso
wrapped in a mink stole, her mother by her side
images that would ambush you at night
in the mind's darkest streets: it could
be you, it is you, who but a freak
would pay to look at us? Those betraying
quick glances, the recoil in the gut
that denies kinship—and reveals it.

We were like children asleep
while a dam breaks. Our screams
only knew joy, as we asked for just
one more turn on the Whip, one last
ride on the roller coaster's waves,
a final swell that would spew us out
weak at the knees and laughing.

The Luna Parks are gone, forgotten
with those bombed houses, but the side
show remains. The freaks' dark parade
goes on, children with chopped-off arms
join the Seal Boy, the Tattooed Man

goes to a gas chamber with a blue
number on his wrist. And still
the calliope's tinny whine keeps on,
the grooved futility of that carousel
turns and turns to nowhere. On the wire
thin acrobats perform for a blind god.

FOR BRENDAN
1/1/2007

What remains
is your smile,
the half-hidden,
fugitive smile
of one who knows
a secret land
where things are simple,
where words
are like clear water,
where a flower
is just perfume
and color, and love
is simply a gladness
in the heart
that exists for itself,
a limpid summer day
that warms, and asks
nothing in return.

Without you
we would have had
no glimpse
of what it means
to walk on the air
of a promise because
it has been given.
We are too clever.
We see the pitfalls
of ambiguities, know
the hollow ring
of counterfeit words.

We are well-armored.
But your world
had no defenses.

Perhaps
Eden was like this.

EXILE AT SARZANA

FLY FISHING—LAKE COMO

My father is fly-casting
at the lake. A snap—the line
whips out graceful and cruel
over still water, a hand-tied lure
dances yellow and red
and weightless, a bright
nasturtium death. "It's all
in the wrist," he explains
as he pulls in a writhing pike,
a skill built on physics
and patience. My father opens
his creel, drops the pike
on a bed of grape leaves.
For a moment he's still, a dark figure
carving the morning's clarity.

At fifty-seven, he's flown planes
in two wars, escaped
from a prisoner's train
and now builds bridges
and loves fishing—and opera. "
"*O patria mia*" he whistles softly
as he casts out, "*mai più, mai più...*"
The line snaps taut—a speckled trout,
this time. The creel's trap door
opens again to the green crypt. Aida
joins Radames in a living grave.

Around the lake September
has turned scarlet the woodbine,
empurpled grapes for the harvest.
In his harvest years, my father

harvests his lake. He doesn't know
he too is caught, the hook
invisible but deep. There'll be
no more Septembers. "*Il sogno
é dileguato,*" my father hums.
"*Mai piú, mai piú.*" Inside the creel
the fish lie quiet in their leafy shroud.

MALLORQUIN

How generous
of this fig tree
that owes me nothing
to hide me from the road,
leaves like webbed hands
hold sunshine
and promises of fruit.
Shadowy patterns
vein my skin with green
filigree. Under
this living tent
Bedouin thoughts
come to rest, August
bleaches the shore.
Through my eyelashes
the sea, hit by the sun
explodes, eyes
drown in light.
Your image fades
to an over-exposed
photograph, edges
no longer cut. Under
the olive trees
a wandering
belled sheep
adds Syracusan
overtones, memories
of sleeping gods,
golden bees.

MONTEROSSO
Cinque Terre

Here where mountains descend,
rock to rock, into a sea
today so quiet, so gray
under the soundless rain
of a precocious September
that it evokes a confluence
of seasons come and gone
and the people you met
along the way (the path
at times easy, at times
as scabrous as the trails
that tie these five villages)
here, today, you feel the past
return: those quiet waves
become time's metronome—and yours.

II

The sun brings back August
with an explosion
of bougainvilleas
against a stucco wall,
red and yellow begonias
fat in their clay pots, basil
on a window sill. Midday,
a man comes by on the beach
selling coconut wedges
in a zinc bucket. He surges
out of time gone, and again
you are a child, that coconut
cool and white as white marble
in your hand—fragment of a past

you thought lost, while
it just went on without you.

Then you know:
what you've been, ends here
at this liquid infinity
so unknowable
it mocks the chances
you still believe in.
You feel diminished
by all you've left undone,
and yet strangely forgiven.

III

The sea assaults the rocks
today, an indigo and white fury
lashes blind at scrubby tamarisks
clinging stubborn to a cliff.
Defenseless lemon trees
tremble in the garden.

Up at the station,
a mournful train
answers the roaring waves
as it pulls away.

TO GUIDO CAVALCANTI
(1259-1300)

I fell in love with you
at thirteen: "Noble, rich, handsome,
sought out by all"
my schoolbook said, "yet of a moody
and solitary nature."
No Hamlet, though: a man of fiery passions
in politics and love.
And a poet! How could I, lost in quagmire
of teen-aged desires,
not be enchanted by this brooding
Florentine prince,
so darkly ardent—and so safely dead?

It would have been
an unrequited yearning: thin, dark, shy,
a twig not yet in bloom,
I would have been content to watch you go
by on the Ponte Vecchio
and feel the pangs of love borne in a glance.
The love of Dante
for Beatrice—where eyes chastely meet
and twin souls commune.

I really wanted happiness
for you alone. I was even pleased
you had a mistress,
Monna Vanna, of such surpassing fair
loveliness she was called
"la Primavera." "She comes and makes the air
tremble with clarity,"
your poem said, and I would see a goddess

go by on the Lungarno,
incarnate spirit of Florence in the spring,
air like colloidal gold,
the river banks abloom with daffodils.

La Primavera! What a dismal
contrast I would have been to so ethereal
a creature. Yet did she
love you as I would have? When you went
heartbroken and alone
into exile at Sarzana, where was she?
How I dreamed I could
go back in time to share that loneliness
with you! Did she grieve
for your fate? In reading your last song,
that "ballad of the exile,"
did she cry—as I did—for all the lost
longings of a life
too soon over? Oh, Guido, love endures.
I'm Autumn, now
and still I'm held in thrall
by love words
you wrote centuries ago, words
fresh and clean as the scent of daffodils.

SCUBA

Oui! Grande mer de delires douée,
Peau de panthère—
    P. Valery
    Le Cimitière Marin

The canopy
of Valery's panther's skin,
a golden fleece
that kills the sun—
zebra skin, rather,
from below,
liquid weight
suspended
like the lead on my belt,
silence,
flicks of fins
and disappear, green
green black
to vanish into,
a thin lifeline of air
rushes skyward in panic
as it should:
temptation is strong here.

We glide newborn
in a lost continent
of winged stillness:
stingrays, barracudas—
coral branches
vibrate to a mute echo
of Triton's horn.
Boundaries between elements
dissolve, primordial silence

dissolves even
the click of the camera.
The roll of pictures
you took of me
showed nothing but green water.
Cameras
don't lie.

OCEAN CITY

The journey
ends here, where it began.

I

How shall we return to the sea
besmirched beyond the boardwalk
by sticky clouds of cotton candy,
T-shirts with "Maryland is for crabs"
stenciled across the chest, the sign
for Blue Horizon Motel insidious waves
licked to ruin last April, how
will we dare reclaim
the silence of the starfish
blood-red against the reef?
Yet our spoor glistens on the sand
—gills to lungs, fins to footprints.

II

Early morning, July, the beach
empty, newly-born. Only an outlaw
black Labrador, drenched and happy,
barks at sandpipers in the waves.
Debris washes in, cuneiform messages
from a cryptic tide. Fragmented
angel wings, bone-bleached driftwood,
broken beer bottles polished to topaz
carry the lesson of all destructions:
in the stilled
song of blue whales
our own end waits.

III

A tribal need brings us all
here, to the edge. Anointed
for a forgotten ritual of renewal
we mimic death, let the midday sun
place copper coins on our eyelids.
In voices eroded by the wind
language reverts, becomes the cry
of earthbound gull, saved—or doomed—
by a lost instinct.

IV

Forecast of storm, the boardwalk
battens its hatches. The sea is lead
lining a coffin, desolation
of funerals in the rain. The sky
presses down in silent judgement.
Then, the wind. Tatar waves
invade the shore, slam the pier,
suck abandoned umbrellas to their doom.
The sea unmasks, a liquid *Dies Irae*
calls back drowned sailors.

V

But in the aftermath a heartbeat tide
ebbs and flows in the blood,
the inner sea calls salt to salt,
brings back the deep, the lost
gills, fin limbs, the swaying
anemone heart. We know you again,
then: we're yours and exiled

forever, wayward castaways
lighting bonfires on a winter
beach, thin air harsh
to sponge lungs, the grit of sand
alien and cold under our new feet.

MEMORIAL DAY, CAPE MAY, 2007

The fog came in from the sea
last night, a silent invasion
conquered the beach, seeped
across the highway into the garden
and in the mist ghosts came back,
memories of other landings—Anzio,
Salerno, Omaha Beach. Revenant
names, empty and pale as shells
left on the wet sand by the tide.

This morning, flags are dimmed
by the fog, droop from balconies,
but grills are readied, picnics
planned. It's the first holiday
week-end at the beach, the sun
surely knows his duty. The past?
The past at times is like a serpent's
outgrown skin, something better shed
along the way. And maybe we need
to forget in order to go on. Then
a fog comes in, blurs the present
in ambiguous nostalgia for what was.

Still, it's a May morning, at Anzio
Roman children splash in the waves
with happy, first-summer feet. "We'll
stop them at the tide line," *il Duce*
had promised on the radio. Maybe
the dead look down and forgive all.

By noon the sun has burned the ghosts
from the sea. Yes, summer is coming,

let the cuckoo sing. Sudden, a phalanx
of black Rolling Thunder motorcycles
roars by the prized Victorian
gingerbread, chrome flashes sharp
as a blade in the sun. Muted blue
and shell-pink, the hydrangeas nod
their heavy balloon heads in the wind.

THE SHAPE OF WATER
(San Giovanni, Lake Como)

A lizard basks on red granite,
its tail a comma between last
and first name. I never knew
this Grandi, Roberto, whose tomb
the lizard is editing, but as I walk
gravel paths among the silent neighbors
of my grandparents' graves, faces,
names surge to greet me. Ginevra,
my grandmother's maid, who could dance
the charleston. Carlo, her carpenter
husband. Tomaso from the sweets shop,
who gave me a candy for each year
on my birthday. And Nino, tall
and thin, who rented boats
at the small harbor by our garden gate.

I recognize them all. But who
were they, these familiar strangers,
the adults of my childhood summers?
I count the decades of their lives
I never knew, carved deep on slabs
and all I hold are labile phantoms
of a past as fluid as this lake
so deceptively unchanged, so still
under the gold of a September sun,
while a river runs cold and unseen
in its depth—glaciers' ice and snow
melted by time, mutating like our lives.

MIGRANTS

Fierce winds scoured the sky clean
last night, the stars' brittle fires
a preview of winter. But this morning
Lake Como shimmers amberine and blue,
and hordes disgorged by the tour boats
wear shorts and sun tops, Nordic flesh
blushing pink in the golden warmth
like a last rose of summer. A blessed
September, after so raw and stormy
an August the swallows abandoned us
on the tenth of the month, streaked away
to kinder skies. An omen, people say.

What's
going on? Subverted seasons, floods,
drought, prices to the stars, one can't
make ends meet. The Italy we knew
is disappearing. Are these swallows
the canary in the mine? They flee
to Africa at mid-summer, and swarms
of Africans come here to litter
our cities with their hopeless need.

Not just them: Albanians, knifers
and pimps, thieving Romanian gypsies,
alien Moslems, Eastern prostitutes.
Night blooming fleurs du mal, an old song
called them. Simpler times. Now they camp
by the highways, patrol our sidewalks,
strut their ware under our children's eyes.
"Mama, what are those ladies doing

in black boots and bikinis? It's evening,
they'll catch cold."

And then the politicians, anointed
thieves, the drugs. How much longer,
Catilina? Enough! Throw them all out,
the brazen crooks, the "*vó cumprá*"
with their strings and umbrellas,
the murderous pimps, pack the Rom
back where they belong. Scour the place
with a fierce, cleaning wind. We want
our country back.

But Italy has always
been invaded: too beautiful, too open
a mirage for vain hopes. So swallows
forsake us at midsummer and hordes
of desperation come. That little
Bulgarian whore strangled and dumped
in the oak woods above the lake
last week—seventeen, her husband
her pimp—last rose of a dreadful
summer, now remains here with us,
cradled dead in the silent leaves,
small lost swallow who didn't leave
our shores, and now is ours,
now finally belongs.

36 NEW ASPECTS OF GHOSTS
Yoshitoshi Taiso

Woodcut #23
The autumn winds blow.
Nothing more left to say.
Grass grows through the
eye sockets of Ono's skull.

The poet stares out
at a gray square space,
tall autumn reeds
sway russet in the wind.
The room is cold. What
is a poet, when he has
no words left? No mist
of melancholy here, only
straight, hard edges
define the hollow moment
when nothing remains.
A faded orange kimono
(his? hers?) hangs empty
in a corner. The past
is gone, futile
to look back. Her skull
is out there, unseen
in the gray wind.
Your fingers touch
that strong, green grass,
cold as the years to come.

KISMET

Yellow crocus
hiding your turban
among the dandelions,

slumming Caliph
roaming at night
Baghdad's seamy streets

in search of a true love,
take heed: fate
plays tricks with dreams.

You might be mistaken
for a weed, tossed
on the compost heap

while the princess
who loves you
waits in the palace

desolate and alone.

OF SAINTS AND SNOWS

The life-size St. Francis
preaching to pigeons,
bronze and real, at the fountain
in the square (the live ones
asleep, puffed up to ruffled
grey balls against the cold)
offered me a friendly blessing
with a hand filled with snow
as I snuck by to meet you.
That candid benediction
gave me hope. Surely
a saint who could tame a wolf
and cared for stupid pigeons
would find a way to rescue
an impossible love.

But we had such a bleak,
soul-searing winter that year,
and even an indulgent saint
can get weary, bare feet
in snow, snow furring his cowl,
trickling down to an emaciated
bronze chest. Perhaps I asked
too much, perhaps I should have
picked a sturdier savior. Now,

I know better. The open wounds
of youth become with time
bloodless and precious
as the bronze stigmata
hidden by that giving snow.
A few flakes in the air

and all comes back: you
and me, and Francis, forever
safe in an endless winter
bitter and sharp and perfect.

GOING BACK

My brain is cosmopolitan:
has traveled to Tibet,
shifts gears smoothly
between four languages,
goes to the opera, reads
Proust in the original,
enjoys fusion cuisine,
gravlax, brut champagne.
But recently my stomach
is turning peasant. It craves
the rustic fare of long-gone
Lombard autumns: polenta
yellow in a copper cauldron,
uncouth mountain cheese tasting
of whey, hot chestnuts swimming
in milk, green and purple figs
fresh from the tree and, like
a greedy child, looks forward
to the squat panettone of yester-
year, to a brittle, hard bar
of *torrone* for Christmas.
Perhaps there is a simple
animal wisdom here, in this
return to comforts one knew,
the acceptance of an ending cycle,
like the dead leaves going back
to earth under a silent
autumn rain, like the earth
preparing for the winter snows.

LETTER TO YANG CHEN CHAI
(1090-1138)

I thought you'd like to know how strong
the permanence of impermanence can be:
almost a thousand years and the footprints
you left with those blue slippers as you stepped
on to a ferry's landing slick with frost
endure. A morning at the Ta Kao gorge
so lost in fog you couldn't see the mountains
nor the river, and only a baying dog—probably
unhappy after a long night out in the cold—
and the crowing from an unseen rooster
helped guide you to the village. A thousand years

and I watch you step out of the page,
endearing traveler from another shore
with those bright blue, upbeat slippers.
And while I think of Charon and his boat,
of whom you knew nothing—any crossing
to an unseen land can feel the same,
doesn't it, in spite of time and different
fogs hiding the path—I have no need
for that unhappy dog nor that rooster,
not with your footprints etched so clear
in virgin frost, and a bright touch of blue.

OPERA BALL AT THE GERMAN EMBASSY

"I'm from Mallorca" the Spanish
ambassador tells me at dinner. Just
a name, and those long-gone summers
flow back unbidden in a golden tide:
amphibious days, the morning sea
like a second skin, smooth, essential,
the sun flaming the air to a mirage
of possibilities, a life outside time,
outside thought. Fringed afternoons
under a canopied fig tree, sharing
the honeyed fruit with drunken bees,
blackberries ripe along white dusty roads,
the scent of wild anise in the wind.
And always the sea, the immensely blue,
embracing sea. Strange how our years
become books we read only once
and store on a shelf. Then, a word,
and days fall out from a random page
like pressed flowers.

At the embassy, together with a table
carved out of ice—salmon sushi, clams—
they've built a an eight-foot replica
of the Berlin wall, in celebration. Twenty
years since it came down. Plaster board
and rough stucco, splotchy red and black
graffiti. Ugly as the real thing, but no
bodies snared on barbed wire. People pose
in front of it, drinking champagne.
A woman admires my gown—perfect
for a summer ball.

Next morning, at the hospice. I change
the dressing on a patient. Cancer
has carved a jagged cave beneath
his jaw, strands of necrotic stalactites
hang down. Burl-knots of fresh tumors
cropped up along the neck, "My ear
feels blocked" he says. "It must
be wax." I nod. We keep no mirrors
at the hospice. I watch the carotid
pulsate exposed, reinforce the dressing.
"Yes," I say. "That wax can really
be a pain." Those Mallorcan days
fill the room. The wall stands there.

ABOUT THE AUTHOR

LAURA BRYLAWSKI-MILLER, who was born and raised in Milan, Italy, holds an undergraduate degree in Allied Health and received an MFA in Creative Writing from American University. She has worked as a Surgical Physician's Assistant, and has published several essays and medical articles. Her work, notable for its elegance and psychological acuity, includes two novels (*The Medusa's Smile* and *The Square at Vigevano*) and a poetry collection (*The Snow on Lake Como*) published by Washington Writers' Publishing House. A new novel (*The Shadow of the Evening*) is forthcoming from Eloquent Books. Miller lives in Arlington, VA and travels frequently between the United States and Italy.